THE WORKPLACE DYSFUNCTIONARY

A Satirical Dictionary of
Workplace Absurdity

ZOË WUNDENBERG

©2025 Zoë Wundenberg. All Rights Reserved.

No part of this publication may be reproduced, stored in a retrieval system, or transmitted in any form or by any means—electronic, mechanical, photocopying, recording, or otherwise—without prior written permission from the publisher, except for brief quotations used in reviews or scholarly work.

ISBN: 978-1-7641006-3-2

First published in 2025 by Impressability.
www.impressability.com.au
Suite 11, 137 High Street
Wodonga Vic 3690
Australia

This book was printed on paper sturdy enough to absorb coffee, tears, and the occasional forehead thump.

For anyone who pushes snooze on their alarm to steal just nine more minutes of peace before rushing off to work—with a sigh in their heart and their hopes in the bottom of their coffee cup— this is for you.

And for Ren. Even though you died. Asshole.

Dysfunctionary

/dɪsˈfʌŋkʃəˌnɛri/ noun

A dictionary of workish words that capture the real emotional experience of work—equal parts satire, survival guide, and sacred text for the professionally exhausted.

> **Origin Note:**
> Born from burnout, forged in WhatsApp and Slack threads, and lovingly compiled by people who know that "professionalism" is just improv. with a dress code.

CONTENTS

Preface.. vii

Micromanage This................................... 1
Words about bosses, hierarchy, and the absurdity of corporate logic.

The Leadership Complex.......................... 7
Power, performance, and the strange rituals of being "in charge."

The Cult of Productivity......................... 13
Hustle culture, toxic optimisation, and the worship of busyness.

I'm Fine. Thanks For Asking.................. 19
Burnout, breakdowns, and the Emotional Labour Olympics.

Inhuman Resources 25
Policies, compliance, and the people-shaped spreadsheet cells.

Pants Optional... 31
Remote life, digital disconnection, and the experience of working from home.

Synergise My Soul................................... 37
Corporate jargon, branding, and the surreal language of work.

Error 404: Motivation Not Found............ 43
Tech, tools, and the digital chaos of modern work.

Reclaiming The Workday......................... 49
Hope, resistance, and the quiet power of saying "No thanks."

Your Own Dysfunctional Words.............. 55

Afterword.. 64

About the Author..................................... 65

Preface

Welcome to The Dysfunctionary—a book for anyone who's ever stared at their screen wondering if work is just long-form improv. with no punchline.

This is not a dictionary in the traditional sense. It's not even in alphabetical order (in true dysfunctional style). It's a survival manual disguised as satire. A collection of made-up words that describe very real feelings, frustrations, and absurdities of modern work life. From Slack sobbing to strategery, from busification to burnout bingo, the entries are here to name what's been unnamed, laugh at what's been endured, and affirm what you already know in your bones: it's not just you.

Whether you're a quietly quitting rebel, a pajamafied Zoom ghost, or a dignity-flexing boundary queen or king, this book is your permission slip to feel seen, laugh loudly, and reclaim your workday—one made-up word at a time.

This book won't fix the system. But it might help you name it, and laugh while you do.

Zoë xx

MICROMANAGE THIS

Management, but make it chaotic.

This section is for those who suffer from bosses who hover, the managers who delegate like confetti, and the systems that confuse control with competence.

Micromanagerie
/ˌmaɪkroʊˈmænəˌʒɛri/ noun

A chaotic zoo of tiny, unnecessary tasks assigned by someone who thinks control equals competence.

Usage:
My inbox is a micromanagerie of redundant approvals and passive-aggressive reminders.

Bossplaining
/ˈbɒsˌspleɪnɪŋ/ verb

When your boss explains your own job to you, incorrectly, with confidence.

Usage:
He bossplained my role to me while mispronouncing the software I built.

Delegasplosion
/ˌdɛlɪɡəˈsploʊʒən/ noun

When a manager offloads everything at once and vanishes like a magician.

Usage:
She dropped a delegasplosion at 4:59 PM and ghosted me.

Visionquesting
/ˈvɪʒənˌkwɛstɪŋ/ verb

Pursuing a "big idea" with no budget, no plan, and no clue.

> **Usage:**
> We're visionquesting a new strategy that's mostly vibes and whiteboards.

Promotastrophe
/prəˌmoʊˈtæstrəfi/ noun

A promotion that turns a decent human into a jargon-spewing haunted shell of their former self.

> **Usage:**
> She used to be grounded and brilliant—now it's all "leverage synergies" and dead eyes. Total promotastrophe.

Leadertainment
/ˌliːdərˈteɪnmənt/ noun

Leadership that prioritises optics, applause, and LinkedIn posts over actual decisions.

> **Usage:**
> Our quarterly meeting was pure leadertainment—no answers, just vibes.

Strategery
/strəˈtiːdʒəri/ noun

A vague, overcomplicated plan designed to sound impressive while accomplishing very little.

> **Usage:**
> We need a new strategery before Q4, preferably with synergy and vibes.

Commandfluencer
/kəˈmændˌfluːənsər/ noun

A manager who leads via motivational quotes and vibes, not actual strategy.

> **Usage:**
> He's more of a commandfluencer than a leader—his entire plan was just a Canva graphic.

KPIsolation
/ˌkeɪpiːˌaɪsəˈleɪʃən/ noun

Being judged by metrics that have nothing to do with your actual work.

> **Usage:**
> I'm in full KPIsolation—my performance review was based on someone else's spreadsheet.

Managerial Drift
/ˌmænəˈdʒɪriəl drɪft/ noun

When a leader slowly loses touch with reality, the team, and the mission.

> **Usage:**
> He hasn't even spoken to us in weeks. He has no idea what's going on—classic managerial drift.

PowerPointification
/ˌpaʊərˌpɔɪntɪfɪˈkeɪʃən/ noun

Turning real work into slides so someone else can pretend they did it. And bore everyone to death with the details.

> **Usage:**
> I wrote the report, she PowerPointified it—and now she's presenting my work with gradients and bullet points.

Leadershipping
/ˈliːdərʃɪpɪŋ/ verb

Performing leadership theatrics without solving problems, making decisions, or showing up.

> **Usage:**
> He's been leadershipping all week—lots of pep talks, zero follow-through.

Chain-of-Commandos

/ˌtʃeɪn əv kəˈmændoʊz/ noun

People who enforce hierarchy with military zeal and zero emotional intelligence.

> **Usage:**
> The chain-of-commandos shut down our idea because it didn't come from above.

Perfommander

/pərˈfɔːmændər/ noun

A manager who commands with flair but no follow-through.

> **Usage:**
> He's a perfommander—great speeches, no decisions.

Titleflation

/ˌtaɪtəlˈfleɪʃən/ noun

Inflating job titles to make people feel powerful while keeping their pay the same.

> **Usage:**
> I'm now a "Senior Strategic Workflow Architect"—titleflation at its finest.

THE LEADERSHIP COMPLEX

Power, performance, and the rituals of being "in charge."

> Here we name the strange behaviours, cycle of meetings, and theatrical decisions that define modern leadership—because if you don't laugh, you'll cry in the breakroom.

Execxiety
/ɛgˈzɛksaɪəti/ noun

The chronic stress of pretending to have a vision while secretly Googling "how to lead."

> **Usage:**
> Her execxiety was palpable—she kept saying 'circle back' while visibly panicking.

Decidophobia
/dɪˌsaɪdəˈfoʊbiə/ noun

The fear of making a decision without a committee, a spreadsheet, and three rounds of feedback.

> **Usage:**
> We've been stuck in decidophobia for weeks—no one wants to sign off.

Leaderloop
/ˈliːdərˌluːp/ noun

A cycle of meetings where leaders talk to other leaders about leading, without touching the actual work.

> **Usage:**
> They're stuck in a leaderloop—four VPs discussing synergy while the project burns.

Visionboarding
/ˈvɪʒənˌbɔːrdɪŋ/ verb

Creating aspirational plans that look great on slides but have no grounding in reality.

> **Usage:**
> We spent three hours visionboarding a strategy that doesn't exist.

Powerfloat
/ˈpaʊərˌfloʊt/ verb

To hover above the team, offering vague encouragement and zero accountability.

> **Usage:**
> He's been powerfloating since the reorg—lots of "great work," no actual support.

Hierarchasm
/ˈhaɪərɑːrkæzəm/ noun

The thrill of enforcing rank, titles, or seating arrangements with unnecessary intensity.

> **Usage:**
> She corrected my email salutation with a full hierarchasm.

Managerial Theatre
/ˌmænəˈdʒɪriəl ˈθiːətər/ noun

The performance of leadership rituals without substance, often involving buzzwords and branded notebooks.

> **Usage:**
> The offsite meeting was pure managerial theatre—no decisions, just matching hoodies.

Coresthesia
/kɔːrɛsˈθiːʒə/ noun

The numbing effect of hearing your company's core values repeated for the 87th time.

> **Usage:**
> I was deep in coresthesia during the all-hands. My brain went numb after the repeated recitation of our "core values" without any attempt to demonstrate them in practice.

Visionvoiding
/ˈvɪʒənˌvɔɪdɪŋ/ verb

The act of generating lofty leadership goals with no plan, no budget, and no intention to follow through.

> **Usage:**
> We spent three hours visionvoiding—now we have a mural and zero deliverables.

Authenticish
/ɔːˈθɛntɪkɪʃ/ adj.

The approved version of authenticity that fits the brand guidelines.

> **Usage:**
> She gave an authenticish speech—relatable, but clearly HR-reviewed.

Visionvertising
/ˈvɪʒənˌvɜːrtəˌtaɪzɪŋ/ noun

Selling a dream that no one internally believes in.

> **Usage:**
> The rebrand was pure visionvertising—big promises, zero substance.

Feedback Fable
/ˈfiːdbæk ˈfeɪbəl/ noun

A mythical tale in which feedback is welcomed, acted upon, and leads to meaningful change.

> **Usage:**
> She told me to be honest—then ghosted me. Classic feedback fable.

Managerial Mimesis
/ˌmænəˈdʒɪriəl maɪˈmiːsɪs/ noun

The tendency of managers to imitate other managers' behaviours, regardless of effectiveness or relevance.

> **Usage:**
> He started using synergy metaphors after that webinar—pure managerial mimesis.

Leadager
/ˈliːdəˌdʒə(r)/ noun

A person who thinks being a manager automatically makes them a leader, while remaining fixated on short-term tasks, metrics, and control—with no investment in the team's growth, wellbeing, or future.

> **Usage:**
> He scheduled daily stand-ups, banned remote work, and called it leadership. Classic leadager.

THE CULT OF PRODUCTIVITY

Words about hustle culture, toxic optimisation, and the worship of busyness.

> This section honours the sacred chaos of optimisation culture, where busyness is worshipped and burnout is rebranded as ambition.

Busyfication
/ˌbjuːsɪfɪˈkeɪʃən/ noun

The process of appearing busy at all times to avoid being assigned more work—or questioned.

> **Usage:**
> I've mastered busyfication. My calendar's full of fake meetings and my Slack is always green.

Grindwashing
/ˈɡraɪndˌwɒʃɪŋ/ noun

The rebranding of burnout as ambition, usually by companies that sell hustle as identity.

> **Usage:**
> Their careers page is pure grindwashing—"We work hard and play harder" is code for no boundaries.

Optimysticism
/ˌɒptɪˈmɪstɪsɪzəm/ noun

The belief that better time management will solve systemic dysfunction.

> **Usage:**
> I bought three planners and still cried before lunch—classic optimysticism.

THE CULT OF PRODUCTIVITY

Gratituduty
/ˈɡrætɪˌtuːdi/ noun

The obligation to express gratitude for toxic workloads, unrealistic expectations, or basic human decency.

Usage:
I sent a thank you email for being allowed to take a lunch break—peak gratituduty.

Inboxhaustion
/ˌɪnbɒksˈhɔːstʃən/ noun

The mental fatigue caused by an overflowing inbox filled with low-stakes chaos.

Usage:
I opened Outlook and felt instant inboxhaustion—47 threads, zero clarity.

Plannertia
/plænˈɜːʃə/ noun

The state of endlessly planning without ever starting.

Usage:
We've been stuck in plannertia for weeks—so many templates, no actual progress.

Focusnomics
/ˈfoʊkəsˌnɒmɪks/ noun

The illusion that productivity can be hacked with timers, apps, and scented candles.

> **Usage:**
> I spent $80 on focusnomics and still got distracted by my own thoughts.

Taskmosphere
/ˈtæskməˌsfɪər/ noun

The ambient pressure of unfinished tasks hovering around you like emotional smog.

> **Usage:**
> The taskmosphere in my home office is suffocating—I can feel my to-do list judging me.

I'M FINE. THANKS FOR ASKING.

Burnout, breakdowns, and emotional labour Olympics.

Here we name the quiet collapses, the performative resilience, and the moments when "I'm fine" is just code for "please send snacks and a therapist."

Smilapse
/ˈsmaɪlæps/ noun

The moment your forced smile collapses mid-meeting and no one notices.

> **Usage:**
> I had a full smilapse during the quarterly review—my face gave up before I did.

Crisistential
/kraɪˈzɪstənʃəl/ adj.

Simultaneously experiencing a personal crisis and an existential one, often during work hours.

> **Usage:**
> I hit a crisistential wall at 2 PM—existence and inbox both imploded.

Breakdownload
/ˈbreɪkdaʊnˌloʊd/ noun

The emotional crash that follows a day of pretending everything's fine.

> **Usage:**
> I scheduled a breakdownload for after my last Zoom call.

Emotivation
/ɪˌmoʊtəˈveɪʃən/ noun

The fragile emotional fuel that keeps you going despite zero actual motivation.

> **Usage:**
> I'm running on pure emotivation—caffeine, spite, and desperation of the eternal pressure to make rent.

Burnoutique
/ˌbɜːrnaʊˈtiːk/ noun

The curated, aesthetic version of burnout that's socially acceptable to post about.

> **Usage:**
> She's in full burnoutique—candles, journaling, and a caption about "rest as resistance."

Therapocalypse
/ˌθɛrəˈpɒkəlɪps/ noun

The emotional unraveling that occurs when your therapist asks, "How have you really been?"

> **Usage:**
> I had a therapocalypse in session three—cried about work, childhood, and my inbox.

Resiliencing

/rɪˈzɪliənsɪŋ/ verb

Performing resilience for others while quietly falling apart.

> **Usage:**
> I've been resiliencing all week—smiling, nodding, and Googling "how to disappear."

Emotional Labour Day

/ɪˈmoʊʃənəl ˈleɪbər deɪ/ noun

A day off that still involves managing everyone else's feelings.

> **Usage:**
> I took an emotional Labour Day—no meetings, just soothing my team's panic.

Caffeindifference

/ˌkæfiˈndɪfrəns/ noun

The state of being too caffeinated to care.

> **Usage:**
> I hit caffeindifference by 11 AM—heart racing, soul flatlining.

Zoompathy
/ˈzuːmpəθi/ noun

The act of pretending to care during a video call while emotionally checked out.

Usage:
I gave great zoompathy during the crisis debrief—nods, mm-hmms, zero retention.

Feelingslide
/ˈfiːlɪŋslaɪd/ noun

The slow descent into emotional chaos while trying to stay professional.

Usage:
I was fine until the feedback session triggered a full feelingslide.

Affirmachanic
/əˈfɜːrməˌkænɪk/ noun

Someone who fixes emotional breakdowns with affirmations, snacks, and memes.

Usage:
She's our team's affirmachanic—keeps us alive with compliments and chocolate.

Exhaustiquette

/ɪgˈzɔːstɪˌkɛt/ noun

The polite way of expressing burnout without making others uncomfortable.

> **Usage:**
> She used peak exhaustiquette—said '"just a bit tired" while her soul left the Zoom.

Performative Fauxkay

/foʊˈkeɪ/ noun

A synthetic version of being okay, deployed for professional survival.

> **Usage:**
> He gave a solid performative fauxkay—cheerful tone, dead eyes.

INHUMAN RESOURCES

Policies, compliance, and the spreadsheetification of people.

This section is for the forms, the feedback loops, and the HR-approved empathy that makes you question if anyone here is okay.

Formageddon

/fɔːrˈmægədən/ noun

The bureaucratic avalanche of forms, surveys, and checkboxes that precede any actual support.

Usage:
I asked for mental health leave and triggered a full formageddon.

Compliants

/kəmˈplaɪənts/ noun

Employees who follow every rule out of fear, not trust.

Usage:
The team's full of compliants—quiet, exhausted, and terrified of HR.

Policyganda

/ˌpɒlɪˈsiːˌgændə/ noun

The cheerful branding of policies that protect the company more than the people.

Usage:
Their "Wellness First" initiative was pure policyganda—no actual changes, just posters.

HRbitration

/eɪtʃˌɑːrbɪˈtreɪʃən/ noun

The illusion of conflict resolution through HR-led meetings that solve nothing.

Usage:
We had an HRbitration about the toxic manager—he's still here, just cc'ing us less.

Onboardoom

/ˈɒnbɔːrˌduːm/ noun

The slow descent into despair during a company's onboarding process.

Usage:
I'm stuck in onboardoom—watched six videos on compliance and forgot my own name.

Feedbackloopiness

/ˈfiːdbækˌluːpinəs/ noun

The surreal experience of receiving vague, contradictory feedback from five different sources.

Usage:
"My review was peak feedbackloopiness—"Be more assertive, but also less direct."

Exiterview

/ˈɛksɪtərˌvjuː/ noun

A final interview designed to collect insights the company will never use.

Usage:
> I gave a brutally honest exiterview—HR nodded and filed it under "misc."

Policyosis

/ˌpɒlɪˈjoʊsɪs/ noun

The condition of creating new policies to avoid addressing real problems.

Usage:
> They responded to the harassment complaint with policyosis—three new PDFs, zero accountability.

Handbookery

/ˈhændˌbʊkəri/ noun

The surreal experience of receiving vague, contradictory feedback from five different sources.

Usage:
> I asked for flexibility and got pure handbookery —"Page 47 says no."

HRnesia
/eɪtʃɑːrˈniːʒə/ noun

The selective memory loss HR experiences when asked about past promises.

> **Usage:**
> They swore we'd get mental health days—now it's all HRnesia.

People Opsychosis
/ˈpiːpəl ˌɒpsaɪˈkoʊsɪs/ noun

The corporate delusion that renaming HR to "People Operations" makes it more humane.

> **Usage:**
> We're still overworked and underpaid, but now it's People Opsychosis.

Humansourced
/ˈhændˌbʊkəri/ noun

Description of a person who's been reduced to a resource, metric, or interchangeable unit of labour.

> **Usage:**
> Ever since the restructure, I've felt totally humansourced—just a metric in someone's dashboard.

INHUMAN RESOURCES

Handbook Drift
/ˈhændˌbʊk drɪft/ noun

The slow, silent shift of policies away from reality, relevance, or anything resembling human experience.

> **Usage:**
> The handbook says we have mental health days—they vanished in Q2. Classic handbook drift.

Empathyload
/ˈɛmpəθiˌloʊd/ noun

The emotional burden placed on employees to be kind, patient, and understanding in systems that aren't.

> **Usage:**
> I hit empathyload—comforted a teammate, coached a manager, and still got ghosted by HR.

PANTS OPTIONAL

Remote work, digital disconnection, and surreal rituals from the couch.

> Here we celebrate the slippers-wearing spreadsheet warriors and the robe-clad rebels who keep the world running from bed.

Zoomnesia

/ˌzuːmˈniːʒə/ noun

The inability to remember anything said during a video call, despite nodding the whole time.

> **Usage:**
> I had Zoomnesia five minutes after the meeting—no notes, just vibes.

Slackrobatics

/ˌslækrəˈbætɪks/ noun

The art of dodging messages, reacting with emojis, and appearing engaged without committing to anything.

> **Usage:**
> I mastered Slackrobatics—three thumbs-up, one gif, zero deliverables.

Pajamafication

/pəˌdʒɑːməfɪˈkeɪʃən/ noun

The gradual blending of work and loungewear until you forget what "real clothes" feel like.

> **Usage:**
> I'm deep in pajamafication—haven't worn pants with a zipper since Q2.

Mute Panic
/mjuːt ˈpænɪk/ noun

The sudden terror that you've been talking while muted —or worse, unmuted and making noise when you weren't meant to be.

> **Usage:**
> I had a mute panic moment after my dog let out a massive gas cloud off-camera and I thought my mic was on! No way would anyone have believed it wasn't me!

Tab Drift
/tæb drɪft/ noun

The slow, unconscious migration from work tabs to irrelevant ones, often ending in existential Googling.

> **Usage:**
> I started with spreadsheets and ended in tab drift— reading about wombats at 11 AM.

Zoomorphing
/ˈzuːˌmɔːrfɪŋ/ verb

Adapting your facial expressions and posture for video calls, while feeling completely dead inside.

> **Usage:**
> I was Zoomorphing all morning—smiling like a hostage, nodding like a bobblehead.

Deskboundaries

/ˈdɛskˌbaʊndəriz/ noun

The invisible line between work and life that no longer exists when your desk is also your kitchen.

Usage:
My deskboundaries collapsed—I answered emails while reheating soup.

Background Anxiety

/ˈbækgraʊnd æŋˈzaɪəti/ noun

The low-level stress of wondering what's visible behind you on camera.

Usage:
I cleaned my room for background anxiety, not inner peace.

Workcrastination

/wɜːrkˌkræsˈtɪneɪʃən/ noun

Avoiding one work task by doing another, less urgent one that feels productive.

Usage:
I spent two hours organising my inbox—classic workcrastination.

Zoomposure

/ˈzuːmˌpoʊʒər/ noun

The fragile state of curating your video call background to appear calm, competent, and not mid-breakdown.

> **Usage:**
> I rearranged my plants for Zoomposure—then cried behind the ring light.

Backdropression

/ˌbækdrəˈprɛʃən/ noun

The creeping dread that your background reveals too much about your emotional state.

> **Usage:**
> My laundry pile triggered backdropression during the team check-in.

Remotivation

/rɪˌmoʊtəˈveɪʃən/ noun

The fleeting burst of energy that comes from remembering you can work in bed.

> **Usage:**
> I had a wave of remotivation—answered five emails under a blanket.

Snackquisition

/snækˈkwɪzɪʃən/ noun

The strategic retrieval of snacks during meetings, often disguised as thoughtful silence.

> **Usage:**
> I made a snackquisition mid-call—muted, nodded, returned with crackers and clarity.

Zoomus Interuptus

/ˈzuːməs ˌɪntəˈrʌptəs/ noun

The unexpected intrusion of real life into a video call, often involving children, pets, or existential chaos.

> **Usage:**
> I was mid-presentation when my toddler burst in wearing a cape—classic Zoomus Interuptus.

SYNERGISE MY SOUL

Corporate jargon, branding, and the language of nonsense.

This section is for the buzzwords, the brandwashing, and the meetings where no one knows what's being agreed to—but everyone nods anyway.

Brandwashing
/ˈbrændˌwɒʃɪŋ/ noun

The act of slapping a feel-good brand message on something soul-crushing.

> **Usage:**
> They brandwashed the layoffs—called it a "values-led transition."

Synergasm
/ˈsɪnərˌgæzəm/ noun

The ecstatic reaction to hearing multiple buzzwords in one sentence.

> **Usage:**
> He hit a full synergasm after someone said "leverage cross-functional ideation."

Jargonosis
/ˌdʒɑːrgəˈnoʊsɪs/ noun

The condition of speaking exclusively in corporate buzzwords, often without realising it.

> **Usage:**
> She's deep in jargonosis—asked me to "circle back with a bandwidth check."

Missionfication
/ˌmɪʃənfɪˈkeɪʃən/ noun

Turning every task into a "mission" to make it sound noble.

Usage:
We're missionficating the Q3 cleanup—because "data hygiene" wasn't inspiring enough.

Thoughtleadiosis
/ˌθɔːtˌliːdɪˈoʊsɪs/ noun

The condition of compulsively posting vague insights online to appear visionary.

Usage:
He's deep in thoughtleadiosis—three LinkedIn posts a day, zero actual ideas.

Valuganda
/ˈvæljuːˌgændə/ noun

The strategic use of company values as emotional manipulation.

Usage:
They used valuganda to guilt us into working weekends—"We're all in this together."

Valueseeking

/ˈvælju:ˌsi:kɪŋ/ verb

The act of searching for meaning in a company's core values and finding only synonyms.

> **Usage:**
> I spent an hour valueseeking—I found out that "integrity" just means "don't get sued."

Buzzword Buffet

/ˈbʌzwɜ:rd bəˈfeɪ/ noun

A meeting or document filled with so many buzzwords it induces semantic nausea.

> **Usage:**
> The strategy deck was a buzzword buffet—"agile," "pivot," "ecosystem," and "value-add."

Strategery Deck

/ˈstrætədʒɚi dɛk/ noun

A PowerPoint presentation filled with vague goals, abstract arrows, and no actual strategy.

> **Usage:**
> We spent two hours on the strategery deck—no plan, just triangles and hope.

Brandemic

/bræn'dɛmɪk/ noun

The uncontrollable spread of brand language into every corner of the workplace.

> **Usage:**
> We're in a full brandemic—my job title is now a "culture catalyst."

Sloganosis

/ˌsloʊɡəˈnoʊsɪs/ noun

The inability to distinguish between real company slogans and parody.

> **Usage:**
> I thought "Empower the Now" was satire—turns out it's our new tagline.

Cultureplaster

/ˈkʌltʃərˌplæstər/ noun

A superficial fix applied to toxic environments using branded values and team-building exercises.

> **Usage:**
> They threw a cultureplaster over the burnout—pizza party, no policy change.

Ecosystemification

/ˌiːkoʊˌsɪstəmɪfɪˈkeɪʃən/ noun

The process of rebranding unrelated tools, teams, or ideas as part of a unified "ecosystem."

> **Usage:**
> They ecosystemified our inbox, calendar, and mood board—now it's a "collaboration hub."

Jargonise

/ˈdʒɑːgənaɪz/ verb

To weaponise the use of jargon in order to overcomplicate communication, assert superiority, and leave others confused, seemingly at their own peril.

> **Usage:**
> He jargonised the whole meeting—by the end, I wasn't sure if we were aligning or ascending, and that lack of clarity is likely to bite me on the butt.

ERROR 404: MOTIVATION NOT FOUND

Tech, tools, and the digital chaos of modern work.

> Here we name the tab-hopping, the apathy, and the spreadsheet-induced existential crises that define our daily grind.

ERROR 404: MOTIVATION NOT FOUND

Appathy
/ˈæpəθi/ noun

The emotional numbness caused by switching between too many apps with no actual progress.

> **Usage:**
> I toggled between five platforms and accomplished nothing—pure appathy.

Tablash
/ˈtæblæʃ/ noun

The mental whiplash from jumping between too many browser tabs.

> **Usage:**
> I had a full tablash—forgot what I was doing and ended up reading about sea otters.

Clicknosis
/klɪkˈnoʊsɪs/ noun

The trance-like state of clicking through digital tasks without absorbing any information.

> **Usage:**
> I entered clicknosis during the compliance training—clicked "next" 47 times, remembered nothing.

ERROR 404: MOTIVATION NOT FOUND

Notificrash
/ˌnoʊtɪfɪˈkræʃ/ noun

The emotional collapse triggered by a flood of notifications across multiple platforms.

> **Usage:**
> Slack, Teams, and email hit me at once—full notificrash.

Lagpathy
/ˈlæɡˌpəθi/ noun

The emotional detachment caused by constant video lag, frozen faces, and delayed reactions.

> **Usage:**
> I gave up mid-sentence—lagpathy took over and no one noticed.

Techtonic Shift
/tɛkˈtɒnɪk ʃɪft/ noun

The sudden upheaval caused by a new tool rollout that no one asked for.

> **Usage:**
> We survived a techtonic shift—new CRM, new chaos.

Platformnesia

/ˌplætfɔːrmˈniːʒə/ noun

The confusion of forgetting which platform holds which task, file, or conversation.

> **Usage:**
> I searched Slack, Notion, and Google Drive—classic platformnesia.

Autoformatastrophe

/ˌɔːtoʊ fɔːrməˈtæstrəfi/ noun

The disaster caused by automatic formatting that ruins your document and your will to live.

> **Usage:**
> My report turned into a bullet-point graveyard—total autoformatastrophe.

Syncxiety

/sɪŋkˈzaɪəti/ noun

The fear that your files, calendar, or brain haven't synced properly.

> **Usage:**
> I had syncxiety all morning—kept refreshing, still missed the meeting.

Cloudfusion
/ˈklaʊdˌfjuːʒən/ noun

The confusion of forgetting which platform holds which task, file, or conversation—caused by too many clouds, not enough clarity. Ironically, actual cloud fusion is what is needed.

> **Usage:**
> I spent 20 minutes searching Slack, Notion, and Drive before realizing the doc was in Dropbox. Classic cloudfusion.

Pingstinct
/ˈpɪŋkstɪŋkt/ noun

The reflexive flinch when you hear a notification sound, even if it's not yours.

> **Usage:**
> I jumped at someone else's Slack ping—my pingstinct is fully conditioned.

Scroll Fatigue
/skroʊl fəˈtiːg/ noun

The exhaustion caused by endless scrolling through irrelevant updates, tasks, or messages.

> **Usage:**
> I hit scroll fatigue by 10 AM—my brain tapped out.

— ERROR 404: MOTIVATION NOT FOUND —

Clustercache

/ˈklʌstərˌkæʃ/ noun

A tangled mess of outdated files, broken links, and conflicting versions that no one can sort out.

> **Usage:**
> The shared drive is a clustercache—three folders named "final," none of them correct.

Syncstorm

/ˈsɪŋkˌstɔːrm/ noun

The chaotic convergence of multiple tools trying to sync at once, resulting in total digital meltdown.

> **Usage:**
> Slack, Google Drive, and Notion all froze—classic syncstorm, followed by a reboot ritual.

RECLAIMING THE WORKDAY

Hope, resistance, and the quiet power of saying "no thanks".

> This section is your rally cry. For boundaries, dignity, and the small acts of defiance that remind you that you are not just a resource. You are a person.

Uncalendaring
/ʌnˈkælənˌdɛrɪŋ/ verb

The radical act of removing unnecessary meetings from your calendar to reclaim your time.

> **Usage:**
> I spent the morning uncalendaring—my soul returned by lunch.

Boundarenaissance
/ˌbaʊndəˈrɛnəsəns/ noun

A personal rebirth sparked by enforcing boundaries at work.

> **Usage:**
> She's in a full boundarenaissance—declining invites and logging off at five.

Nope Cycle
/noʊp ˈsaɪkəl/ noun

The empowering loop of saying no, feeling relief, and doing it again.

> **Usage:**
> I entered a nope cycle—declined three meetings and felt reborn.

RECLAIMING THE WORKDAY

Out-of-Office Alchemy
/ˈaʊt əv ˈɒfɪs ˈæl.kə.mi/ noun

The transformation that occurs when you truly disconnect and remember who you are.

> **Usage:**
> I set my email auto-reply and felt the out-of-office alchemy—suddenly I had thoughts again.

Task Divorce
/tæsk dɪˈvɔːrs/ noun

The intentional separation from tasks that were never yours to begin with.

> **Usage:**
> I filed a task divorce—stopped doing my manager's emotional labour.

Replentitlement
/ˌriːplɛnˈtaɪtəlmənt/ noun

The radical belief that rest is not earned, but required.

> **Usage:**
> I'm practising replentitlement—napping without guilt, logging off without apology.

Quiet Quittique
/ˈkwaɪət kwɪˈtiːk/ noun

The artful, intentional withdrawal from overwork, disguised as professionalism.

> **Usage:**
> She's mastered the quiet quittique—meets expectations, protects her peace.

Boundary Audit
/ˈbaʊndəri ˈɔːdɪt/ noun

A review of where your time, energy, and dignity are leaking.

> **Usage:**
> I did a boundary audit—found three meetings and a Slack channel to delete.

Calendar Cleanse
/ˈkælənˌdər klɛnz/ noun

The ritual of removing meetings that do not serve your soul.

> **Usage:**
> I performed a calendar cleanse—my week now has oxygen.

Reorgproof

/ˈriːɔːgˌpruːf/ adj.

Describing a boundary so strong it survives any reorganisation.

> **Usage:**
> My Fridays are reorgproof—no meetings, no chaos, just me.

Soulbandoning

/ˈsoʊlˌbændənɪŋ/ verb

The act of leaving behind roles, tasks, or identities that no longer serve your spirit.

> **Usage:**
> I'm soulbandoning the hustle—I'm choosing rest. I'm choosing me.

Declinergy

/dɪˈklaɪnɚdʒi/ noun

The surge of energy that follows saying no to something that drains you.

> **Usage:**
> I felt pure declinergy after skipping the all-hands meeting—suddenly I could breathe again.

Restpect

/ˈrɛstˌpɛkt/ noun

The act of honouring someone's need for rest without guilt, judgment, or productivity shaming.

> **Usage:**
> She logged off early and I sent her a heart emoji—full restpect.

Unburnout Plan

/ʌnˈbɜːrnaʊt plæn/ noun

A personal strategy for undoing the damage of chronic overwork, often involving naps, boundaries, and snacks.

> **Usage:**
> My unburnout plan includes deleting Slack, buying candles, and never saying "circle back" again.

ADD YOUR OWN DYSFUNCTIONAL WORDS

ADD YOUR OWN DYSFUNCTIONAL WORDS

ADD YOUR OWN DYSFUNCTIONAL WORDS

ADD YOUR OWN DYSFUNCTIONAL WORDS

ADD YOUR OWN DYSFUNCTIONAL WORDS

ADD YOUR OWN DYSFUNCTIONAL WORDS

ADD YOUR OWN DYSFUNCTIONAL WORDS

ADD YOUR OWN DYSFUNCTIONAL WORDS

ADD YOUR OWN DYSFUNCTIONAL WORDS

Afterword
For the Gloriously Burned Out

This book is for the ones who've smiled through breakdowns, nodded through nonsense, and quietly reclaimed their dignity one boundary at a time. It's for the survivors of onboarding mazes, Slack avalanches, and synergasmic strategy decks. It's for anyone who's ever whispered "I'm fine, thanks for asking" while Googling "how to disappear professionally."

> You are not alone.
> You are not just a resource.
> You are not a calendar slot.

You are a whole human—with thoughts, thresholds, and a right to rest.

So here's to the quiet rebels, the affirmachanics, the uncalendarers, and the ones who've mastered the art of saying "no" with a smile. May your inbox be light, your boundaries be reorgproof, and your soulbandoning be complete.

About the Author
Zoë Wundenberg

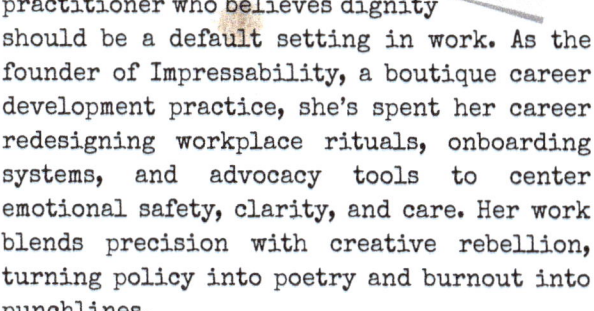

Zoë is a systems-loving, satire-slinging careers practitioner who believes dignity should be a default setting in work. As the founder of Impressability, a boutique career development practice, she's spent her career redesigning workplace rituals, onboarding systems, and advocacy tools to center emotional safety, clarity, and care. Her work blends precision with creative rebellion, turning policy into poetry and burnout into punchlines.

She's mentored teams, coached leaders, and built tactile resources that feel like a warm hug in a world of cold emails. Whether she's naming the absurd, sketching layout ideas, or troubleshooting a binding machine at midnight, Zoë brings rigor, wit, and deep compassion to everything she touches.

This book is her love letter to the gloriously burned out, the quietly defiant, and the ones who keep showing up with snacks, spreadsheets, and soul.